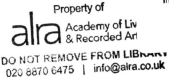
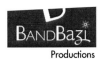

Productions

Tells the stories that connect people

MIND WALKING
BY TANIKA GUPTA

Bobbie | Peter D'Souza
Moira, his wife | Kate Dyson
Rosa, his daughter | Philippa Vafadari
Matty, his grandson | Tarrick Benham
Aerial Technician | Jonothan Campbell

Directed | John Binnie
Designed | Ellen Cairns
Choreography | Philippa Vafadari
Lighting Design | Chris Williams

Poster and Leaflet Design | David Churchill
Production Manager | Marcia Stephenson

There will be no interval

Mind Walking was originally developed with the British Council UK-India Connections through Culture programme and was commissioned by BandBazi with the assistance of Arts Council, England. It was originally co-produced with Q Theatre Productions, Mumbai.

Since Philippa Vafadari started the company in 2001, BandBazi (Farsi: *Trapeze*) has gained national and international status for creating new writing that is immediate and innovative and responds imaginatively to contemporary issues. The company is a forerunner in the evolving art form of Aerial Theatre fusing breathtaking aerial circus with compelling story lines and fully fleshed characters. It won an Edinburgh Fringe First for New Writing in 2005 for its production *Breakfast at Audrey's*.

Mind Walking has given the company the opportunity to further push the boundaries of the form and strive for excellence in this subtle and exacting genre, where the balance between skills and storyline has to be perfectly pitched and where gratuitous 'tricks' cannot take precedence over the emotional impact of the narrative drive. BandBazi's narrative-driven work fits into the exploration of aerial circus and theatre by a number of high-profile practitioners, including the RSC's Shakespeare Histories cycle; *Romeo & Juliet* (Playhouse Theatre) and *Metamorphosis* (Lyric Hammersmith). However, *Mind Walking* is innovative within Aerial Theatre in that Tanika Gupta was specifically commissioned with the aerial metaphor in mind making it one of only a handful of proper plays written by a respected living playwright that fuses aerial circus with a strong character-driven storyline that resonates with emotional truth.

www.bandbazi.co.uk; mail@bandbazi.co.uk;
0044 1273 240918; 0044 7803 451530

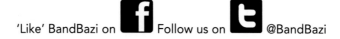

'Like' BandBazi on ▮ Follow us on ▮ @BandBazi

The UK Premiere of *Mind Walking* was at Watermans Theatre, Brentford on 29 September 2011

The Indian Premiere of *Mind Walking* was at the Delhi International Arts Festival on 8 November 2011

A scratch performance of *Mind Walking* was presented at The Alchemy Festival, Southbank Centre in April 2010.

ORIGINAL Cast and Crew included

Matty, his grandson | Dylan Kennedy

Assistant Director | Quasar Thakore Padamsee
Production Manager | Greg Mickelborough
India Team | Alan Tweedie

BandBazi would like to thank:

Abhishek Saha, Adam Pushkin, Alex Poulter, Anne and Shahrokh Vafadari, Basel Zaraa, The Board of BandBazi, Brighton Youth Centre, Corrado Cigna, Darius Shroff, David Fielder, David Burns PR, Dinyar Tirandaz, Erica Dellner, Ervad Rustam Bedvar, the Ferdowsi Trust Fund, Hannah Jarman, Harminder Berman, Hardish Virk, Ian Lawton, Jehangir Sarosh, Karla Singh, Karoki Mahmoodi, Malcolm Deboo, Marian and Tehmtan Framroze, Mari Binnie, Matt Costain, The Nehru Centre, The Nightingale Theatre, Oscar Robinson Alam, The Point Eastleigh, Preeti Gaonkar, Robin Mitchell, Rusi Dalal, sam-culture, Sam Kerawala, Sammy Bhiwandiwalla, Shahvir Irani, Sorab Ardershir, The Southbank Alchemy Festival, Toral Shah, Umesh Patel, Veronica Dewan, Vicky Long, the World Zoroastrian Organisation and the Zoroastrian Centre, London

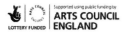

BandBazi is a registered charity no: 1091276

TANIKA GUPTA is an acclaimed British playwright and TV dramatist. She has written for National Theatre, Young Vic, Royal Court Theatre, and the RSC. She received the Arts Council John Whiting Award for her play *The Waiting Room* in 2000, the Asian Women of Achievement Award 2003 and the Amnesty International Media Award 2005. Her new play, *The Empress* will open the 2013 Spring Season for the Royal Shakespeare Company.

JOHN BINNIE is a writer/director with Glasgow's Clyde Unity Theatre. His productions have won three Edinburgh Fringe First Awards and the Independent Theatre Award. He has toured productions in the United States, Namibia, Nigeria, Singapore and Germany. He is currently developing a new musical *Heart Songs* and is reviving his play *Killing Me Softly* for The New Wolsey Theatre, Ipswich. John has extensive experience of teaching playwriting with community groups.

ELLEN CAIRNS studied at Glasgow School of Art and The Slade in London. She won the Arts Council Theatre Design Bursary in 1981 and has been designing extensively in this country and abroad since. Recent productions include *Spin the musical*, in Shanghai, *Les Miserables* and *Cabaret* in Finland, *Rainman* and *Taking Sides* in Estonia, *Private Lives* and *A Raisin in the Sun* at Manchester Royal Exchange, *The New World Order* at Brighton Festival and *One Flew Over the Cuckoo's Nest* in Leicester. She previously collaborated with BandBazi on *Love Indeed*.

PETER D'SOUZA trained at RADA. Among other roles he has played King Lear, Polonius and Claudius in *Hamlet*, Sir Toby Belch in *Twelfth Night* and Elliot in *Private Lives*. Film and TV roles include roles in *The Loneliness of the Long Distance Runner*, *633 Squadron*, *Madame Bovary*, *The Mill on the Floss*, *For Whom the Bell Tolls* and *The Saint*. He previously taught at the Royal Scottish Academy of Music and Drama for over thirty years before joining Theatre Babel as dramaturg and actor.

KATE DYSON trained at Guildhall School of Music and Drama. Theatre credits include Lady Bracknell in *The Importance of Being Ernest*, Elderly Woman in *New World Order* (both for the Brighton Festival), Madame de Volange in *Les Liaisons Dangerous* (West End and World Tour), Maria Josepha in *The House of Bernarda Alba* (for The London Shakespeare Workout). As well as numerous roles in West End musicals and for the National Theatre, Kate spent two years with The D'Oyly Carte Opera Company.

PHILIPPA VAFADARI trained at The Scottish Royal Conservatoire and The Circus Space, London. She has worked extensively as both an actress, aerialist and choreographer. Her self-penned, *Pussy Galore's Flying Circus* (BandBazi) received critical acclaim at the Edinburgh Fringe Festival and she played Audrey/Holly in BandBazi's Edinburgh Fringe First Award-winning *Breakfast at Audrey's* as well as creating the roles of Elizabeth/Cleopatra in the recent tour of *Love Indeed*. As 'Mary Poppins', Philippa was one of the specialist aerial performers at Danny Boyle's Opening Ceremony for the London 2012 Olympic Games.

TARRICK BENHAM started his training at the National Youth Theatre of Great Britain. He has since graduated from Arts Educational Schools London. His drama school credits include: Orlando in *A Midsummer Night's Dream*, Peider The Soldier in *Andorra* (Directed by Maria Aberg), and Mark in Mike Bartlet's *13*. He is also a member of 'Gorilla Productions' film production company.

JONOTHAN CAMPBELL Is the Artistic Director of Aye! Productions which has produced two shows *Sealskin Trousers* and *The Ballad*. He was Aerial Designer/Technician for Catherine Wheels, Claire Cunningham, Communicado, Company Chordelia, Gravity and Levity, Michael Clarke, The National Theatre of Scotland, V.amp Productions and Yes No Productions. He was stunt co-ordinator for Grid Iron's *Decky Does a Bronco*, performed in The National Theatre's production of *Jumpers* and directed Leo Kay and the London Philharmonic Orchestra in a homage to Charles Chaplin.

MARCIA STEPHENSON graduated from Middlesex University with a degree in Drama and Theatre Studies in 1992. Based in London, she has travelled all over the UK, Europe and worldwide working with numerous touring theatre, aerial dance, circus, site-specific, pyrotechnic and live event companies. Most recently, she was production manager for the Little Angel Theatre/Kneehigh production *A Very Old Man with Enormous Wings*.

CHRIS WILLIAMS has more than 20 years experience in live theatre both as Production Manager and Lighting Designer, working on a range of productions from rock concerts to stand-up comedy. He was head of the technical department at The Komedia Brighton, before moving to run the Sallis Benney Theatre at Brighton University. He previously worked with BandBazi as lighting designer for *The Persian Cinderella*.

DYLAN KENNEDY's theatre credits include *The Beauty Queen of Leenane* (Royal Lyceum, Edinburgh), *'Peter Pan* (National Theatre of Scotland), *All Over Town* (Calipo Theatre), *A Skull in Connemara* (Love and Madness), *Alice in Wonderland* (Theatre Royal, Portsmouth), *Hansel and Gretel* (National Theatre). His screen credits include Graham Norton in *The Young Graham Norton* for Channel4, *Inside Outside* with LoveLovisa Films and *Liam in Plasticine* with Kollage Films.

QUASAR THAKORE PADAMSEE has directed and produced over 20 plays with the Mumbai-based theatre company Q Theatre Productions. He also works as lighting designer, stage manager, conducts workshops and is a passionate crusader for the survival of theatre in the public consciousness. He is one of the founders of Thespo, a youth theatre movement, which culminates in a festival each December in Mumbai. It is now in its 13th year.

GREG MICKLEBOROUGH has worked as a technician, stage manager, and production manager for several touring companies, festivals, and theatres, including Electric Voice Theatre, BBC Proms 2009, Ragroof Theatre, The Two Wrongies, Bryony Kimmings, and 30 Bird Productions. Greg was the former Venue and Technical Manager of The Basement theatre in Brighton, works very closely with the Nightingale Theatre, and is the Production and Stage Manager for Festibelly music festival.

ALAN TWEEDIE's theatre career stretches back to the 70s with 7:84 Theatre Co. Through the 80s and early 90s he was managing Theatre Workshop Edinburgh during its heyday as producing theatre and welcoming host for the best of small-scale touring theatre. Since mid-90s Alan has had a wide portfolio of arts development experience with increasing focus on the south Asian sub-continent. He now has work and homes in two continents.

MIND WALKING

Tanika Gupta

MIND WALKING

OBERON BOOKS
LONDON

WWW.OBERONBOOKS.COM

First published in 2013 by Oberon Books Ltd
521 Caledonian Road, London N7 9RH
Tel: +44 (0) 20 7607 3637 / Fax: +44 (0) 20 7607 3629
e-mail: info@oberonbooks.com
www.oberonbooks.com

A catalogue record for this book is available from the British
Library.

PB ISBN: 978-1-84943-506-2
E ISBN: 978-1-84943-820-9

Cover design by David Churchill

Printed, bound and converted
by CPI Group (UK) Ltd, Croydon, CR0 4YY.

Visit www.oberonbooks.com to read more about all our books
and to buy them. You will also find features, author interviews and
news of any author events, and you can sign up for e-newsletters
so that you're always first to hear about our new releases.

Characters

BOBBY (SORABJI)
Elderly Parsi man in his 70s

ROSA
40-year-old woman. Bobby's daughter, Aerialist.

MATTY
16-year-old youth. Bobby's grandson, Aerialist

MOIRA
Bobby's wife. 60s

SCENE 1

The Sunset Nursing Home.

We create the soundscape of a busy nursing home: elderly people laughing, crying, shouting etc. BOBBY is standing next to his bed getting dressed. He is elderly but looks sturdy.

He is putting on a shirt, smart jacket and tie but has his pyjama bottoms on. BOBBY gets into a tangle with the tie, gets it all in a terrible knot. Eventually exhausted with the effort, he collapses in a chair and sulks.

BOBBY: *(Calls out.)* Moira? Moira! Can you help me with my tie? Moira?! I'll be late for work.

There is no response.

A shaft of light streams through the window on to him. BOBBY squints into the light and shields his eyes. Slow movements as he reaches out, almost stroking the light beam.

The circeau comes down and BOBBY stares at it confused. The circeau hangs and sways. It seems to captivate BOBBY who slowly stands on shaky legs and reaches out his hand towards it. As the circeau twirls teasingly it makes BOBBY dizzy and he sways as if he is about to fall. MOIRA bustles in. She is a cheerful, elderly Scottish woman.

MOIRA: Bobby!

MOIRA manages to steady BOBBY.

MOIRA: You okay?

BOBBY nods and points at the circeau.

MOIRA: *(Laughs.)* What?

Yes, a lovely sunny day. I'll wrap you up nice and warm and take you out for a walk. Okay pet?

MOIRA picks up a blanket and arranges it on BOBBY's lap.

MOIRA: Look at your tie! And you don't have your trousers on!

MOIRA laughs as BOBBY looks down at his pyjamas confused.

MOIRA: You silly sausage.

MOIRA busies herself untying BOBBY's tie and doing it up for him. He sits and allows her.

MOIRA: Terrible traffic this morning – stand still on the flyover. Next time, I'm going 'round the long way. Hate to think of you sitting here waiting for me.

BOBBY: I can't find my briefcase.

MOIRA: What do you need your case for?

BOBBY: I have to get to work! I'm late! Bad traffic you say? Do you have the car keys?

MOIRA: Oh pet…

BOBBY: You've hidden my briefcase haven't you? I have patients waiting for me.

MOIRA looks at BOBBY, upset.

MOIRA: You have the day off today – remember? We're going for a lovely walk.

BOBBY: I don't have to go to surgery?

MOIRA: Not today darling.

BOBBY stares at the circeau again. MOIRA looks up.

MOIRA: What are you looking at old man eh?

MOIRA stares but can't see the circeau.

MOIRA: I have to get someone to change your sheets… Do me a favour will you? Just stay put Bobby. Don't want you having another fall do we?

MOIRA strokes BOBBY's head affectionately. He smiles up at her.

MOIRA looks momentarily sad and then bustles off again.

BOBBY continues to stare at the circeau.

He sees a childlike WOMAN leap and swing into the circeau. BOBBY stands delighted.

ROSA: Dad!

BOBBY: Rosa, I need to tell you something.

ROSA: Come and play Dad.

BOBBY: No, I can't, I need to…

ROSA does a few turns within the circeau. BOBBY watches her amazed and sits down again in his chair.

BOBBY: Listen, I can feel it slipping from me.

ROSA: What's slipping?

BOBBY: Can't remember…

ROSA: Doesn't matter.

BOBBY: Like a black hole, sucking me in.
  I've been jettisoned into a worm hole.

ROSA: In a rocket!

BOBBY: Yes.

ROSA: Whizzing into outer space.

BOBBY: Something like that. You understand, don't you?

ROSA: Not really.

Both BOBBY and ROSA laugh.

ROSA: Does it matter?

BOBBY: I think it does. But I'm not sure.

  Sort of labyrinthine corridors in my head. So many rooms.
  Some full of light, some with all my old friends, some full
  of hills, rolling away from me like waves. Some rooms –
  just empty echoey caves.

ROSA: Dad – you're babbling.

BOBBY: Am I?

ROSA: What are you talking about?

BOBBY: Things are changing.

My mind is walking, leaving me. And there's something important I need to tell you.

ROSA: What?

BOBBY looks away, confused again.

ROSA: Dad. Why don't you come and join me? C'mon! You can decide to walk through any door you like.

BOBBY: I can't.

ROSA: Why not?

BOBBY: I can't.

ROSA disappears.

BOBBY: Wait! Rosa – don't go! There's something I haven't told you!

BOBBY stares at the empty circeau as it swings.

BOBBY sits and stares at the circeau.

Soundscape as we hear various voices coming from the circeau like echoes from the past.

WOMAN'S VOICE: Mix, blend in but stay who you are.

CHILD'S VOICE: Baba! Look at me!

MAN'S VOICE: Face the direction of the sun, if the sun has set, then face the south, but never face the north.

WOMAN'S VOICE: Women in the UK are so easy. Just look at them and they open their legs.

WOMAN'S VOICE: I love you.

MAN'S VOICE: Good thoughts, Good words, Good deeds.

WOMAN'S VOICE: What we want from life and what we get.

Remember! 'Happiness unto him who gives happiness unto others'.

MAN'S VOICE: Good thoughts, Good words, Good deeds. *Humata, Hukhta, Huverishta.*

The empty circeau swings invitingly – BOBBY reaches out as these words and phrases are repeated again and again until eventually they fade. (BOBBY intermittently speaks in Parsi Gujarati.)

BOBBY: Thirty per cent of the blood pumped through the heart in one minute passes through the body's chemical factory, which is called the liver… The liver is located at the top of the abdomen, just below the diaphragm.

… The man that came in was a different person to the one ten years ago… The liver also receives bright red blood from the lungs filled with vital oxygen to be taken to the heart…red blood…that man entirely different from thirty years ago…the liver cleanses the blood and processes nutritional molecules which are distributed to the tissues. Always changing…a chameleon… Another world… I turn around and everyone's gone. Where are they? Abandoned! And who were they?

The only part of the body that receives more blood than the liver is the brain. Not enough blood going to the brain…not enough oxygen…suffocation…slow asphyxiation…brain tissue shrinkage…nerve cells dying… enlarged ventricles…slowly…slowly disappearing…

BOBBY turns and sees MOIRA. He reaches out to her.

BOBBY: This place smells strange. I want to go home.

MOIRA turns away upset.

SCENE 2

MATTY (16) slouches in a chair glued to a smart phone, typing. ROSA enters carrying a basket of washing. She stops for a moment and looks at MATTY. MATTY doesn't look up.

MATTY: Putting some washing on?

ROSA: Yes.

MATTY sniffs his fleece and pulls a face. He quickly peels it off and throws it into the basket ROSA is carrying.

MATTY: Good shot!

ROSA, a little annoyed, marches out with the basket. MATTY laughs at the screen.

MATTY: Nob head!

ROSA: *(Off)* What?

MATTY: Not you, mum. Mate…on FB…posted a really stupid picture of himself.

MATTY continues to chuckle. ROSA re-enters.

ROSA: I wish you'd get out more Matty. Always glued to that tiny screen.

MATTY: Costs money to go out.

ROSA: Get involved.

MATTY: Please.

ROSA: What happened to your girlfriend?

MATTY: *(Groans.)* Ohhh…

ROSA: All your friends?

MATTY: They're still there…just taking a break from them.

ROSA: Your dad and I…

MATTY: I know.

ROSA: It's just a trial separation.

MATTY: You don't need to keep going on.

ROSA looks away. She finds her handbag and starts to put some lipstick on.

He's taking me to the Arsenal match on Saturday.

ROSA: That's nice.

MATTY: And then we're going out for a meal. Think I'll stay over at his.

ROSA: Okay.

MATTY: Mum, when you say 'trial separation', when does it stop being a trial and become fact?

Just be nice to know.

ROSA: I can't give you a date.

MATTY watches as his mum puts on a jacket and searches her pockets for car keys.

MATTY: Where are you off to now?

ROSA: To see your gramps.

MATTY: Piss and crap and boiled cabbages.

ROSA: Don't use that foul language.

MATTY: Urine and excrement then. Whatever you call it, that place stinks.

ROSA: Matty!

MATTY: Last time we went, he was wearing a nappy. He stank. Like he was sat in his own…

ROSA: He's incontinent. It's a good home and they change him regularly.

MATTY: He's all on his own.

ROSA: He can make friends…

MATTY: Make friends with a bunch of old tossers? They're all just as confused as he is.

ROSA: Mum can't look after him anymore.

MATTY: I would have looked after him. I told you.

ROSA: And what about school? You have to study. He needs 24-hour care. I couldn't look after him. And your gran just couldn't do it anymore.

ROSA holds back the tears.

MATTY: Why couldn't she get a nurse?
Someone to help?

ROSA: He didn't take to anyone. He threw his shoe at the last one! Broke her glasses.

MATTY: She deserved it though. She was nasty and rough and she had dog breath.

ROSA can't help but laugh.

MATTY: I miss Gramps. You know what the statistics are for estranged fathers having contact with their kids? One in four lose contact.

ROSA: You won't lose contact.

MATTY: How do you know?

ROSA: I know.

ROSA looks at MATTY with feeling.

SCENE 3

MOIRA and BOBBY are feeding the ducks. BOBBY is enjoying himself lobbing bits of bread at the birds. He is well dressed in his suit and tie now. He laughs happily. MOIRA smiles.

MOIRA: You're like a kid! Ohhh careful of that swan – he's got a mean look in his eye. They can be vicious you know.

BOBBY steps back a little.

MOIRA: Remember that time Rosa was in her push chair and we were feeding the ducks and that swan tried to attack her! She was just a wee girl.

BOBBY continues to throw bits of bread.

MOIRA: You ran forward and kicked the swan – so hard – it hopped and hobbled back into the lake. I was worried you might have broken the bird's neck…but it was alright.

BOBBY stops for a moment and watches a gaggle of geese as they honk and fly overhead. MOIRA looks up too. She takes BOBBY's hand momentarily and kisses it. He smiles at her.

BOBBY: Moira – my love.

MOIRA: Yes – Bobby – my love.

BOBBY: Where are we?

MOIRA: We're in your…in the…

MOIRA looks away, upset.

The Golden Sunset Home for the Elderly.

BOBBY: Are we visiting someone here?

MOIRA: *(Guilty.)* Yes, yes, we are.

BOBBY looks up and sees the circeau again. He walks up to the circeau and touches it, twirling it and playing with it.

MOIRA: What is it you're looking at pet?

BOBBY: It looks like a door.

MOIRA can't see anything.

MOIRA: Where are you going?

BOBBY: Just a minute, I'll be back.

MOIRA calls out as she steps back into the shadows.

MOIRA: Bobby? Bobby!

BOBBY is on his own with the circeau. He stares and marvels at it.

NB: This is the first time we step into BOBBY's 'Alzheimer's world'. It has its own soundscape and atmosphere.

The circeau is lowered enough for BOBBY to step through it. He is immediately transported into another world. We hear the drone of Parsi chanting/praying. Incense fills the air.

BOBBY is delighted – a child again.

BOBBY: Good thoughts, Good words, Good deeds.

MATTY enters dressed as a PARSI PRIEST. He carries a fire which he places in front of them.

MATTY/PARSI PRIEST: Life is a continuous war between the forces of light and the forces of darkness. Good will win if people do good deeds, think good thoughts and speak well.

MATTY/PARSI PRIEST gives BOBBY a piece of thread, he ties it around his waist, tying and untying it again and again as he speaks. He instructs BOBBY as they tie and untie in unison.

MATTY/PARSI PRIEST: Face the direction of the sun, if the sun has set, then face the south, but never face the north. Place the right hand index finger on your navel, look at the floor and think.

BOBBY does the action and chants with the priest.

BOBBY: *Ahura Mazda is Lord! Ahriman he keeps at bay, he holds him back. May all enemies be defeated! I am contrite for all sins and I desist from them, from all bad thoughts, bad words and bad acts which I have thought, spoken or done in the world.*

I praise Asha!
Ashem Vohu.

BOBBY turns to the PRIEST.

BOBBY: I never told anyone that I am a Parsi.

MATTY/PARSI PRIEST: Today is your Naojot. Today you become an adult, responsible for your own salvation. You have a new set of clothes including a sacred thread and shirt and we will sprinkle you with coconut, raisins and almonds for your prosperity. And here is a sacred fire burning fragrant with frankincense and sandalwood.

BOBBY: Why do we need fire?

MATTY/ PARSI PRIEST: Fire symbolises light. Your ancestors took the fire from Iran, in the ninth century. Uprooted themselves and moved to a different world to save their religion. Escaping persecution.

We had to leave. The Muslims in Iran – taxes, public humiliation, taunting…and the Christians destroyed our fires and desecrated our temples.

The circeau is lit up again as we hear the sounds of people screaming and shouting, waves and sea.

MATTY/PARSI PRIEST: Our ancestors landed in Gujarat where the King Jadi Rana had a reputation for fairness that preceded him.

BOBBY sits on the park bench as if it were a throne.
MATTY/PARSI PRIEST pays his respects to him.
(Together they re-enact Parsi legend/history.)

MATTY/PARSI PRIEST: Oh King, we ask you a favour.

BOBBY: Ask and I will decide.

MATTY/PARSI PRIEST: We have come from far where we have been persecuted by the evil ones. We request asylum and a place to worship.

BOBBY: But look at this.

BOBBY cups his hands to denote a bowl.

This vessel of milk is filled to the very brim. My kingdom is already crowded and cannot accept refugees.

MATTY/PARSI PRIEST sprinkles something in the bowl.

BOBBY: What is that?

MATTY: Sugar, your Majesty. We will not bring the vessel to overflowing but instead will make the lives of your citizens sweeter.

BOBBY smiles (as the King).

BOBBY: You Parsis are wise. You may stay, provided you adopt our language, that your women wear the sari and that you henceforth cease to bear arms.

MATTY/PARSI PRIEST: We will be your loyal servants my wise king.

MATTY/PARSI PRIEST bows.

MOIRA: *(OS.)* Bobby! Bobby!

MATTY/PARSI PRIEST walks back through the circeau taking the fire with him and exits. BOBBY follows him back through the circeau.

As he walks back through, MOIRA is waiting for him. He blinks at her, confused.

MOIRA: You disappeared. Where did you go?

BOBBY turns to MOIRA excited.

BOBBY: Good thoughts, Good words, Good deeds.

MOIRA: Good words?

BOBBY: Good thoughts, Good words, Good deeds!

MOIRA tidies BOBBY's hair.

MOIRA: That's a nice saying. Come on pet. Let's get back now.

MOIRA takes BOBBY by the arm and leads him away. BOBBY turns to look at the circeau before exiting.

SCENE 4

Lights up on: the old people's home.

ROSA is trying to feed BOBBY. He sits like a baby, with a bib around his neck although he still has his shirt and tie on underneath.

He eats, slurps, dribbles and grunts. ROSA coos.

ROSA: There, Hmmm…yummy…

I cooked it especially for you…just as you like it…eat up…

MATTY and MOIRA are standing to one side watching.

MATTY: How's he been?

MOIRA: He's getting worse. Wandered off into these bushes on his own, muttering away…I lost him for a full fifteen minutes. Then I found him standing beneath these trees, staring around him wildly, like a child, like he'd seen something…

MATTY: Poor Gramps.

MOIRA: He's slipping away from me. Everyday.

MATTY: Like going backwards.

MOIRA: Says the strangest of things.

BOBBY continues to eat in the background.

MOIRA: My husband, the successful doctor… He's completely batty.

MATTY: But he always was a crackpot.

They both laugh. BOBBY looks across up at them both.

BOBBY: Are you two laughing at me?

MOIRA: No, pet, just…

BOBBY: I know what's happening to me.

MATTY: What's happening Gramps?

MATTY approaches BOBBY.

BOBBY starts talking very fast.

BOBBY: Plaques and tangles in the brain…I know my condition…loss of neurons and synapses in the cerebral cortex and certain subcortical regions.

ROSA: You're blinding me with science now.

BOBBY: Alzheimer's, I have Alzheimer's. I know! I've seen it hundreds of times in my patients. Plaques and tangles in the brain. It's degenerative. Impairments in semantic memory…episodic memory…sometimes total loss of vocabulary or speech…plaques and tangles in the brain…

ROSA: Dad…

BOBBY: I have the diagnosis. I know what the problem is. But I don't have a cure!

No, no cure.

ROSA: Finish your food Dad. You've lost weight. You're not eating properly.

ROSA offers him some food. BOBBY gulps back the food obediently.

The circeau is lowered and BOBBY stares at it. ROSA tries to feed him but he closes his mouth and purses his lips like a petulant baby.

ROSA: Come on Dad.

BOBBY pulls a disgusted face and pushes away the food.

BOBBY: Disgusting, tasteless muck.

ROSA: But it's your favourite!

BOBBY: I hate it.

ROSA: No you don't.

They have a tussle and BOBBY refuses the food.

BOBBY: I want to go – out. *Mane bar javuch.* I want to have a sweet lassi with rose water. I want to feel the sun on my skin. *Mane mara mona par tarku joech.* I'm always so cold here. Never enough blankets.

ROSA looks at MOIRA confused.

BOBBY: No one to talk to. I fall asleep and I keep wondering where I am… *Mane Ainjch Vichaar Aavya Karech, Ke Un Kaan Choun?*

ROSA: Dad…we're all here, me, Mum and look there's Matty over there.

BOBBY: You're very pretty but I'm not sure we've met. Let me introduce myself. *Mane maari orkhan karva do.* How do you do. I'm Bobby Sorabji. *Un bobby sorabji.*

ROSA: No, you mean Bobby De Souza and I'm your daughter.

She points at herself.

Rosa De Souza.

BOBBY looks at ROSA confused.

BOBBY: De Souza? *D'souzi?*
No…
What is my name? *Maru naam su chen?*
Oh dear. *Ooh, khodaie!* Who am I?

BOBBY gets up and walks around agitated. ROSA tries to grab hold of him but he flinches.

28

MOIRA: He's getting agitated now…best to leave him be when he gets like this.

ROSA: He doesn't even recognise me.

MATTY: What did he say his name was?

BOBBY: Sorabji! Bobby Sorabji.

ROSA: No, it's De Souza.

MATTY: Maybe he'll recognise me…
Hi, I'm Matty De Souza. Your grandson.

BOBBY points at MATTY.

BOBBY: Stop playing games with me. I know you're not called Matty. What sort of a name is that? You're Farhad. *Mane maalum chen, taru naam matty nathi, farhad chen.*

ROSA: Dad!

MATTY: Wait, let's hear what he has to say.

ROSA: How can he suddenly say his name's Sorabji?

MOIRA: He's Parsi.

ROSA looks stunned.

MATTY: What's a Parsi?

MOIRA: It's an ancient religion.

MATTY: He changed his name?

MOIRA: Yes.

ROSA: And you never thought to tell me?

MOIRA: It was his wish. I tried to persuade him but he said it was for the best.

ROSA: Mum! I can't believe this.

BOBBY comes up to MATTY and hugs him fondly.

BOBBY: Farhad, I've missed you so much. *Farhad, main tane bau yaad kidu.* Why didn't you ever visit me before?

MATTY: This is really doing my head in.

ROSA: Who the hell is Farhad?

MATTY: Bobby, who's Farhad?

MOIRA: His brother.

ROSA: But he's an only child!

BOBBY: Pulling my leg again – huh? You always were the joker. Farhad, it's me – look! Have I changed so much? Lost my hair a little but still the same face!

MATTY: Cool, he thinks I'm his brother!

Gramps, what's a Parsi?

ROSA: Stop playing games Dad.

MATTY: Just go with it Mum.

BOBBY looks at ROSA and clasps her hands to him.

BOBBY: *Mamma.*

ROSA: Mamma?

BOBBY suddenly gets down on his knees, puts his head in ROSA's lap and hugs her legs like a child.

BOBBY: *Mamma, main tamune bau yaad kidaa.* I missed you so much. Why didn't you ever write me? *Etla badhaa varas sudhi.* All those years. So much anger. *Kaain?* Why?

ROSA looks emotional.

BOBBY: Thank you for coming. *Mane ammesa maalum atu ke un tamune pacho malas.* I always knew I would see you again. How is father?

ROSA: Mum?

MATTY: Ha! He thinks you're his Mum! Cool.

BOBBY: I always wanted to go home and see you, I missed Bombay so much.

MOIRA: He seems very upset… Bobby, maybe you need to rest for a while…

MOIRA helps BOBBY up and guides him to a chair.

MOIRA: You're getting overwrought. Now sit down here and I'll get you a drink…some juice…

ROSA gets up and walks away. She is emotional.

BOBBY is upset. He reaches out to ROSA with outstretched arms.

BOBBY: *Mamma* please don't walk away from me again. I'm so sorry *Mamma* so sorry…

MATTY: What's he sorry about?

ROSA: Dad! What's wrong with you? Why are you making things up?

MATTY: Why would he lie?

ROSA: Why would he hide the truth?

BOBBY: You should have met my wife…you would have loved her…

ROSA: It makes no sense!

MATTY: Mum, Gramps is trying to tell us something. Why won't you listen?

ROSA: He's raving.

MOIRA: No Rosa. Sometimes, people remember things from a long time back.

ROSA: But this changes everything. Who I am, who Matty is… everything.

BOBBY takes ROSA's hand. She snatches her hand away.

Dad, you're being ridiculous.

ROSA exits very upset. BOBBY watches her go – distraught.

MOIRA: You stay with your grandfather. I'll go and see she's okay.

MATTY is left with BOBBY who looks upset.

MATTY: Calm down Gramps.

BOBBY: That's what always happens – see? She gets upset and walks away. Refuses to listen. Refuses.

MATTY: Does that mean I'm a Parsi as well?

BOBBY: Now, she won't talk to me...she won't hear me out... no compromise...everything has to be done according to tradition...how can you live like that? With so many rules? Farhad, you understand don't you?

MATTY: Gramps...what's going on in that head of yours?

The circeau is lowered to ground level now. BOBBY stares at it again. Suddenly he jumps up, like an excited child and starts to take off his trousers.

MATTY: Gramps?

What are you doing?

BOBBY strips down to his vest and shorts. He giggles and rushes towards the circeau. MATTY watches him amazed.

BOBBY walks up to the circeau and peers mischievously through it, as if seeing if the coast is clear. He gestures urgently at MATTY to join him. BOBBY steps through the circeau into 'Alzheimer's world' again. This time we hear the soundscape of children laughing and playing, water splashing, birdsong etc.

SCENE 5

MATTY/FARHAD is on the circeau and is doing elaborate moves to show he is clambering and climbing through the branches of a tree. BOBBY watches him and calls out.

BOBBY: Be careful Farhad! Don't fall or Mamma will kill us both!

Can you see the witch?

FARHAD cranes his neck to look in the distance.

FARHAD: It's okay. She's snoozing in a chair on the verandah.

BOBBY: If the old witch sees you, she'll set those ugly dogs on us.

FARHAD: I'm not scared of those stupid dogs.

BOBBY: You should be. Teeth like razors.

Took a chunk out of Nadir's backside last week.

FARHAD: Pssst… Bobby! Look at these! Ripe.

BOBBY: *(Points.)* That one! Get that one!

FARHAD crawls across the branches and throws mangoes down.

BOBBY: Catch!

BOBBY catches them.

FARHAD: One more!

FARHAD reaches for a last mango and then jumps down to join BOBBY.

They slurp and feast on the mangoes together.

BOBBY: Hmmm…

FARHAD: So juicy.

BOBBY: She'll kill us if she sees us.

FARHAD: Just eat and stop worrying, old man.

The mango juice dribbles down their arms as the two chomp their way through the fruit.

BOBBY: Look, who's this?

BOBBY takes two mangoes and places them on his breasts. He bats his eyelashes and sings a Hindi film song in a high-pitched voice. He prances about like a Hindi film actress. FARHAD laughs uproariously.

FARHAD: Nargis! Ohhh…give me a squeeze of your titties!

FARHAD tries to grab the mangoes. He chases after BOBBY.

BOBBY: Get off!

They fall about laughing and giggling.

BOBBY: Remember Nargis in *Mela*, she was divine.

FARHAD: A Goddess.

BOBBY: Those eyes, like almonds. Her lips…ohhh…I would sell my soul to be Dilip Kumar kissing that mouth.

FARHAD: Even her feet are perfect.

BOBBY: Her feet?

FARHAD: Haven't you noticed her feet when she's dancing – with the nupur tinkling away?

BOBBY: I'm too busy concentrating on other parts of her body.

FARHAD: Check out her feet next time. Beautiful.

BOBBY: I will.

BOBBY and FARHAD go into a reverie for a moment. BOBBY burps loudly and then FARHAD burps too.

BOBBY: Beautiful mangoes.

FARHAD: Best mangoes in the whole of Bombay.

BOBBY: Whole of India!

FARHAD: The world!

BOBBY: The Universe!

Suddenly there is the sound of dogs barking.

FARHAD: Shit! Those ugly dogs! They're coming.

BOBBY: Can't catch us!

FARHAD: Bobby, quick! The witch is coming as well.

FARHAD climbs up the circeau again, swinging adroitly through the branches. The sounds of the dogs gets louder. He helps BOBBY through the circeau and they get away just in time. The dogs are on the other side, slavering and growling, furious.

FARHAD and BOBBY laugh uproariously and make faces at the dogs.

FARHAD: Can't catch us, can't catch us. Stupid bitches.

BOBBY: Stinky breath. Mongrel mutts.

FARHAD: Ugly witch!

BOBBY: Wart-faced crone!

FARHAD: Fat pig.

FARHAD and BOBBY make pig noises, laugh and exit back through the circeau. As BOBBY re-emerges on the other side of the circeau, he stands alone and shivers. MATTY re-enters as himself. He picks up BOBBY's clothes and holds them out to him. BOBBY looks at MATTY confused.

MATTY: Gramps, what's a Parsi?

SCENE 6

ROSA is on the circeau. She looks troubled.

MOIRA enters and watches her.

MOIRA: So?

ROSA: What?

MOIRA: What's going on with you and Mike?

ROSA: He's staying in a friend's spare room, half a mile away.

MOIRA: Poor Mike.

ROSA: Poor Matty.

MOIRA: And you? How are you?

ROSA: Relieved not to be arguing all the time. But it's strange not having him around.

MOIRA: Is it fixable?

ROSA doesn't answer.

MOIRA looks at her troubled daughter.

ROSA: Matty's hurting.

MOIRA: Strange that we've both ended up single women – at the same time?

ROSA: Are you lonely?

MOIRA: Are you?

Started going out again, seeing my friends, still do my yoga…feel guilty.

ROSA: Why?

MOIRA: Like I'm making a new life without him.

ROSA: You have to Mum.

MOIRA: It's not the same without him.

ROSA: Dad doesn't recognise me, thinks I'm his mother. Doesn't even remember his own name. He said he was a Parsi.

MOIRA: Yes.

ROSA: How could you hide such a thing from me?

MOIRA: I didn't hide it – he did.

ROSA: But why?

ROSA is hanging upside down in the circeau. She looks upset.

MOIRA looks up at her.

MOIRA: It was a different world back then. He seemed almost ashamed of his heritage.

ROSA: What was he ashamed of?

MOIRA: I don't know.

He's still your father.

ROSA: I want my dad back. I want my dad.

MOIRA: Stop it.

How do you think it is for me?

How do you think I feel?

MOIRA's voice catches as she fights back tears.

MOIRA: This isn't easy for me you know Rosa.

ROSA climbs down and holds her mother tight.

MOIRA: My Bobby. He was such a clever man and now look at him. The man I've loved for fifty years suddenly transformed into a different person. I can't even look after him anymore. Can't do it, can't manage him…sometimes he becomes a complete stranger.

ROSA: I just wish he'd told us.

MOIRA: He had secrets.

ROSA: I still don't get it.

MOIRA: Get over it will you? We all have secrets. You didn't even tell me about Mike moving out.

ROSA: That's different.

MOIRA: Is it?

ROSA: I still don't get what's going on with Dad.

MOIRA: Don't know if we'll ever find out. His mind's so jumbled up. Don't know what's truth and what's fantasy.

SCENE 7

MATTY is helping BOBBY to dress into his night clothes: pyjamas, dressing gown and slippers.

MATTY: So, I looked up your name – Sorabji – on the internet.

BOBBY is quiet.

MATTY: Yes, you're a Parsi which is Zoroastrian and I discovered…loads of famous people with the same name…

BOBBY: We used to have picnics on Juhu beach…

MATTY produces a piece of paper from his pocket and reads from it.

MATTY: Juhu? Juhu beach? That's in Bombay – right? Anyway, there's someone called Cornelia Sorabji…she was the first woman ever to read law at Oxford back in the nineteenth century!

BOBBY: Monogrammed napkins and when we went up to the Malabar hills, our cows were sent up a month before, so we would have fresh milk. Mamma had an armour guard and real pearls sewn into her shawl.

MATTY: Right. Then there was this other Sorabji…can't
say his first name…anyway, he was a famous pianist
and a composer…apparently wrote really long, difficult
compositions that no one could play!

BOBBY: What happened to those pearls?

MATTY: Hmm…not sure…but listen…and then I found out
that Freddie Mercury was a Parsi!

BOBBY: 'Bohemian Rhapsody'…

MATTY: Yes! Yes Gramps – Exactly. How cool is that? Freddie
Mercury! I never knew that!

MATTY sings a little bit of 'Bohemian Rhapsody'.

'Anywhere the wind blows, doesn't really matter to me…'

BOBBY: Anywhere the wind blows…

MATTY: And I found out Parsis lay out their dead in this place
called the Towers of Silence…and that vultures come and
eat their corpses… That's so weird!

BOBBY: Good thoughts, Good words, Good deeds.

MATTY: I made contact on Facebook with a Sorabji in
Mumbai.

We've been chatting online.

*MATTY tries to tie BOBBY's dressing gown belt for him but BOBBY
takes the belt off him.*

BOBBY: Life is a continuous war between the forces of light
and the forces of darkness. Good will win if people do
good deeds, think good thoughts and speak well.

*BOBBY plays with the belt and ties it around his waist, tying and
untying it again and again as he speaks.*

MATTY watches him.

BOBBY: Face the direction of the sun, if the sun has set, then
face the south, but never face the north. Place the right

hand index finger on your navel, look at the floor and think.

I praise Asha!
Ashem Vohu

MATTY: Anyway, Gramps…this Sorabji said he knew your family. Isn't that amazing?

BOBBY: No family left.

MATTY: Really?

BOBBY: …I met Noël Coward once, he was writing *Private Lives.* He was very rude to my mother but he was such a snappy dresser.

MATTY: Who's Noël Coward?

BOBBY does a quick rendition of 'Mad Dogs and Englishmen'. MATTY laughs and enjoys the song.

BOBBY: Our servant, Joguda, he would press my feet whenever I wanted it.

MATTY: Sounds like your family were rich.

BOBBY: They wasted so much money. All down the drain. Our deaths outweigh our births. We're all dying out. Hardly any Parsis left, because of me.

MATTY: Ah – so it's all your fault.

BOBBY: They brought the fire with them to India to keep our faith alive, to put it in the temple. The Hindus were good to us.

MATTY steadies BOBBY who seems to be swaying.

MATTY: How come you gave it all up? Changed your name – pretended you were someone else?

BOBBY looks away upset.

MATTY: Why didn't you tell me? Or even Mum? What happened to you?

BOBBY is silent. He looks up and sees the circeau lowered again. He walks towards it, climbs through it again.

This time in 'Alzheimer's world' we hear the soundscape of the port/ harbour – boat horns, the sea, people…

BOBBY stands and stares up at the circeau and waves.

MATTY climbs up into the circeau. He swings on it, vigorously, young, full of life, whooping.

As MATTY swings from the circeau, ROSA joins him. BOBBY waves at them both. We hear the sound of a steamer ship blasting its horn.

FARHAD: Bon voyage Bobby! Bring me back
English marmalade jam and Johnny Walker whiskey.

ROSA: *Chup! (Quiet)* – whiskey?!
Bobby! Look after yourself. And write often.
Every day!

BOBBY: I will Mamma!

ROSA: Mix, blend in but stay who you are.

FARHAD: Greta Garbo!

ROSA: Remember! 'Happiness unto him who gives happiness unto others.'

I love you Bobby.

BOBBY: Love you too.

FARHAD: Don't forget us!

BOBBY: I'll be back.

ROSA: Don't forget who you are. You know what they say –
Women in England are so easy – too easy.

FARHAD: Lucky devil.

ROSA: *Chup!*

FARHAD: Bring me back an English princess with golden hair.

ROSA: *(To FARHAD.)* Golden hair eh? Wait 'til I tell your father.

You'll have white hair by the time he's finished with you.

BOBBY laughs and waves.

BOBBY: Goodbye!

ROSA: Good thoughts, Good words, Good deeds.

The steamer ship horn sounds. BOBBY waves and watches as MATTY and ROSA/MAMMA disappear from sight. We hear the sound of the sea and seagulls above. BOBBY stands and takes his ease, savouring the fresh sea breeze.

MATTY re-enters as himself. He watches his grandfather with interest.

BOBBY walks back through the circeau. He stands and looks lost.

MATTY: Gramps? You okay?

BOBBY: I never saw them again.

MATTY: That was the last time?

BOBBY: Went back once, when was it?

MATTY: I don't know.

BOBBY: Can't remember. Everyone gone.
Everyone turned their faces away from me.
Even my brother Farhad.
They scratched me out of their photo albums – that's what I heard. Like I never existed. No trace of me.

MATTY: Why?

BOBBY: Why? Why?

BOBBY starts to weep inconsolably. MATTY tries to comfort him, to no avail. MATTY sits with BOBBY as BOBBY cries.

SCENE 8

It is night time now. BOBBY is sat on his own now, staring ahead of him, quiet, alone and deep in thought, dressed in his pyjamas and dressing gown. He hears the faint echo of an old song – something of its time in the early 1960s. BOBBY hums along to the song a little and then he falls asleep in his chair, nodding off slowly. The circeau appears lit up and we hear the old song getting louder as ROSA swings and somersaults joyously through it, dream-like. Eventually BOBBY awakens and gazes happily up at ROSA.

ROSA: Dad! Dad! Come and play.

BOBBY sits up and giggles.

ROSA: Come on, what are you waiting for?

BOBBY walks across to the circeau. He laughs and plays some sort of a game with ROSA, where he tries to catch her. He chases her and makes grabs at her, tries to tickle her, reach her. ROSA laughs.

ROSA: Can't catch me! Slow coach!

BOBBY chases ROSA through the circeau and into 'Alzheimer's world'. We hear the soundscape of a hospital. ROSA exits laughing.

MOIRA enters. She is dressed in a nurse's uniform. She stands on the other side of the circeau.

BOBBY sees her and watches her with interest. MOIRA busies herself looking through a file. BOBBY quickly tiptoes back to his bed, pulls a blanket up over him and pretends to be asleep. ROSA exits.

MOIRA approaches BOBBY and glances through her notes.

BOBBY opens his eyes.

MOIRA: Ah – Mr Sorabji – you're awake.

BOBBY: Nurse Murdoch.

MOIRA: I don't think we've met before.

BOBBY: What does the M stand for?

MOIRA: Sorry?

BOBBY: On your name badge it says Staff Nurse M Murdoch.

MOIRA: Never you mind.

BOBBY: Where have you been all my life?

MOIRA: Now don't get fresh with me.
    How are you feeling today then?

BOBBY: Much better now – thank you.

MOIRA: Where are you from?

BOBBY: Bombay.

MOIRA: India? Very exotic.

BOBBY: And where are you from?

MOIRA: Glasgow. Not so exotic.
So, according to these notes, you have pneumonia Mr Sorabji!

BOBBY: Caught a chill, then a chest infection…now I'm laid up here.

MOIRA: And you're an important person. You've got a star on your notes.

BOBBY: A Star of David?

MOIRA: No. Are you Jewish?

BOBBY lifts the blanket to inspect himself.

BOBBY: Not the last time I looked.

MOIRA: *(Laughs.)* Stop it!
A star in here, means you're an important patient.

BOBBY: Really?

MOIRA: Yes. What makes you special?

BOBBY: You tell me nurse M Murdoch.

MOIRA: Why have you got a star on your notes?

BOBBY: Because, as you say – I'm special.

MOIRA: Ah! Now I see! You're a doctor.

BOBBY: Nearly qualified – not quite there yet.

MOIRA takes BOBBY's vitals – temperature, pulse etc. BOBBY gazes at MOIRA in total admiration.

BOBBY grasps MOIRA's hand.

MOIRA: What are you doing?

BOBBY: I'm a palm reader.

MOIRA: I have a lot of patients to be seeing Dr Sorabji.

BOBBY: Please call me Bobby.

MOIRA: Bobby, I don't have time for…

BOBBY reads MOIRA's palm.

BOBBY: One child.

MOIRA: Really? You can tell that?

BOBBY: Very clear.

BOBBY: And you're going to leave home.

MOIRA: Already done that.

BOBBY: One broken heart

MOIRA: Done that too.

BOBBY: When?

MOIRA: You tell me. You're the fortune teller.

BOBBY: Erm…three years ago?

MOIRA: Spot on.

BOBBY: Impressed?

MOIRA: Very.

BOBBY: The silly man who broke your heart, whoever he was, he lost out…it says here… One husband.

MOIRA: Only one?

BOBBY: Oh yes. And you'll marry for life.

MOIRA: How dull.

BOBBY: And you're just about to fall in love with a tall foreign gentleman.

MOIRA: Right.

BOBBY: Head over heels.

MOIRA: What's he like?

BOBBY: Gentle, sweet, but very passionate.

MOIRA: Passionate eh? What does he look like?

BOBBY: Devastatingly handsome.

MOIRA: Sounds wonderful. Can't wait to meet him.

There is a beat as BOBBY holds MOIRA's look until eventually, she breaks away, embarrassed.

BOBBY: I can make predictions as well as read palms.

MOIRA: Can you now?

BOBBY: I predict that you and I will be married before the end of the year.

MOIRA: I can't marry you!

BOBBY: Why on earth not?

MOIRA: Because – I haven't seen the world yet. I need to travel.

BOBBY: We can travel together.

MOIRA: Listen pet. I only just escaped from the clutches of my folks. I'm not ready to settle down.

BOBBY: Who said anything about settling down?

MOIRA: You just asked me to…

BOBBY: So marry me and I'll take you to India.

MOIRA: Marriage is a patriarchal institution based on the subjugation of women.

BOBBY: Marx?

MOIRA: No – Engels.

BOBBY: Your life will be different. With me, it will be exciting.

MOIRA: I can't believe we're having this conversation.

BOBBY: I'm going to take you back to Bombay, meet my parents. They'll love you. We'll go for picnics on Juhu beach, watch the sun set over Malabar hills and take a trip to the Elephanta caves.

MOIRA: You are a mischief maker Mr Sorabji.

BOBBY: Please, call me Bobby.

MOIRA: And you can call me Nurse Murdoch. Now, please, rest.

MOIRA bustles off. BOBBY watches her go.

SCENE 9

MATTY is looking through some photo albums. He giggles to himself. ROSA is sorting through some of BOBBY's clothes and dumping them into a suitcase.

ROSA: So many clothes!

MATTY: What are you going to do with it all?

ROSA: Mum wants me to take them down to the charity shop. Dad always was a hoarder. Half of these things haven't been worn in decades. Look at this!

ROSA holds up a particularly psychedelic shirt from the 1970s.

I don't remember Dad ever wearing this.

MATTY: Hey I like that!

ROSA looks doubtful.

I'll have it.

ROSA laughs and throws it across to MATTY. He holds the shirt up against himself and admires it.

MATTY: Cool.

ROSA looks unconvinced.

MATTY: Some great old photos here Mum. Found it at the bottom of Gramps' cupboard. Gran and Gramps on their wedding day. You as a baby. You were a chubby bubby.

ROSA walks over to have a look.

ROSA: Do you mind?!

They both look through the photos.

MATTY: None of Gramps when he was growing up in India.

ROSA: Look how young Mum looked. And Dad…

MATTY: Handsome wasn't he?

ROSA: *(Laughs.)* So much hair! Oh look…

MATTY: Who's this?

ROSA: I've never seen that photo before.

MATTY: Looks faded – Gramps as a baby and his mum?

ROSA and MATTY stare at the photo.

MATTY: She looks like you.

MATTY takes the photo out of the album and puts it in his pocket.

MATTY: You and Dad on your wedding day.

ROSA looks at the picture sadly.

ROSA: We look so happy.

MATTY: You look in love.

ROSA turns away upset.

Dad misses you.

ROSA: Does he?

MATTY: He's waiting for you to call him.

ROSA: It's best you don't get involved Matty.

MATTY: This affects me too you know. I'm the one who has to watch my mum and dad both, separately, sad.

ROSA strokes MATTY's hair.

ROSA: I'll call your dad soon. I promise.

MATTY looks satisfied.

MATTY: Gramps said he met Noël Coward.

ROSA: What?

MATTY: He was famous wasn't he?

ROSA: Just a little bit.

MATTY: Talks about Gran. How she was a nurse and he was a patient with pneumonia.

ROSA: That's true.

MATTY: I wish you'd sit with him and listen. It's fascinating.

ROSA: I find it hard. Why didn't he tell *me* any of this before? Why now?

MATTY: Ask him!

ROSA: I remember this one incident. When I was a kid, I used to get taunted in the playground. They said I smelt of curry.

MATTY: Creeps.

ROSA: I told Dad and he was furious. Marched up to the school and made a terrible scene. Gave the teacher a lecture on Indian history.

MATTY: I can imagine him doing that.

ROSA: I'd never heard him talk like that before. So after, I asked him. Kept asking him. What was it like in India? Who were my grandparents? Was your dad a doctor? Where are our ancestors from?

MATTY: What did he say?

ROSA: 'Your grandparents were simple people, lived by the sea – both died young and I came to be educated in England… no brothers or sisters…no ties back home'.
But now, I discover everything he said to me was a lie.

MATTY: Maybe they were painful memories.

ROSA: He's a hypocrite! He tells me to be proud of who I am
– but he abandoned his family, his religion…

MATTY: But it's exciting Mum! Like a mystery.

ROSA: I can't deal with any of this.

MATTY: Mum. *I'm* supposed to be the teenager.

ROSA looks at MATTY, surprised at first, and then smiles.

*She holds MATTY's hand, descends from the circeau and goes to join
BOBBY.*

SCENE 10

*It is morning. As BOBBY sleeps in his chair, ROSA enters. She watches
her sleeping father and sits down next to him. She takes out a book and
reads. Eventually BOBBY wakes.*

BOBBY: Where am I?

ROSA: You're in the Golden Sunset nursing home.

BOBBY: Have I come to see some patients here?

ROSA: Not today. You're just resting here for now.

BOBBY: Where's Nurse Murdoch?

ROSA: You mean Mum… Moira?

BOBBY: Where is she?

ROSA: She's on a break.

BOBBY: Oh. Has that little girl recovered okay? Surgeons took
a huge tumour out of her stomach.

ROSA: She's doing just fine.

BOBBY: Such a sweet child. Such an innocent face.

You know I met Noël Coward once – he came to dinner.
He was writing *Private Lives*. He was very rude to my
mother but he was very dashing.

ROSA: Dad.

BOBBY: Dad?

ROSA: I'm your daughter.

BOBBY: Pretty girl.

ROSA: Do you know me?

BOBBY: I know that I love you.

BOBBY reaches out and touches ROSA's face. There is momentary recognition.

BOBBY: We called you Rosa because you were born when our garden was full of roses. You filled our lives with sweetness and light.

ROSA: Oh Dad! You do remember me.

BOBBY: My mind is walking. I don't remember things.

ROSA: Don't worry, that's why I'm here.

BOBBY: My mind wanders in and out, all over the place. Little snatches of light and then plunged back into a foggy cave. I am a nuisance to you.

ROSA: No. But it must be so confusing.

BOBBY: Like staring down into a deep well…something moves way below and I strain to see…then I realise it's my own reflection.

ROSA: Dad, can I ask you, why didn't you ever go back – to India?

BOBBY: I tried to. Once. I don't remember when. They were angry…they turned their faces away.

ROSA: Who was angry?

BOBBY: They turned their faces away.

ROSA: Are you talking about your family?

BOBBY: They were angry with me. And I was furious with them.

BOBBY suddenly gets agitated.

Inbreds. Closed-thinking, snobs, inhuman Crazies! Fanatics! Think you're all so special…little private club…a lost tribe. That's all you are! Not even enough people left to call you a religion.

I don't pray anymore. I don't believe anymore. You say I've lost my soul. You say I don't belong but I don't care. I don't care!

BOBBY starts to pace. ROSA watches him.

ROSA: Dad, calm down.

BOBBY turns and looks at ROSA.

BOBBY: I fled from persecution…took the fire with me to another country…

ROSA: What fire?

BOBBY: The fire within me. I took it and carried it within me.

BOBBY sits down. He is quiet.

BOBBY: They never forgave me, I never forgave them.

ROSA: I'm trying to understand Dad.
What made you hide who you were?

The circeau is lowered and BOBBY stares at it.

ROSA: What are you staring at Dad?

ROSA stands and looks in the direction of the circeau.

ROSA: What is it?

BOBBY: A door. It opens and then closes. I go in, I go out.

ROSA: When you go through this door, what do you see?

BOBBY: My world.

MATTY and MOIRA enter and stand on the other side of the circeau.

BOBBY puts his hand out to ROSA. She takes his hand hesitantly and follows him through the circeau.

BOBBY embraces MOIRA. They laugh.

BOBBY: Hello wife.

MOIRA: Hello husband.

They embrace and laugh again, both looking happy. They have a little dance together.

As they embrace, MATTY and ROSA climb up into the circeau.

BOBBY and MOIRA come out of the embrace and both of them walk to stage right and stage left to make a phone call.

ROSA plays the part of BOBBY's mother – MAMMA from the circeau.

MATTY plays the part of MOIRA's father – CLIVE.

BOBBY: Mamma? Mamma! Can you hear me?

ROSA/MAMMA: Yes. Bobby! How are you?

BOBBY: I'm fine Mamma.

MAMMA: I've been so worried – no letter, no calls for months and months…

BOBBY: I had my exams and then I got a new job…

MAMMA: Are you earning well?

BOBBY: It's not bad. Long hours in the hospital. But I am officially a doctor now.

MAMMA: I am so proud of you. My heart is bursting. Doctor Sorabji.

BOBBY: *(Giggles.)* I know, sounds so strange.

MAMMA: You must come home soon though. We will go to the fire temple and give our thanks. We'll have a big party for you… When are you coming home?

We cut to: MOIRA on the other side of the stage who is talking to her father.

MOIRA: Father?

CLIVE: Moira, is that you?

MOIRA: How are you?

CLIVE: Same old. Your mother's not in – I'll tell her you called.

MOIRA: Wait, I wanted to tell you something.

CLIVE: Me?
What's going on?
You okay? You sound a bit strange.

MOIRA: I'm fine Father, in fact, I'm more than fine.

MAMMA: Come as soon as you can…

MOIRA: There's something rather wonderful I wanted to tell you.

CLIVE: Wonderful? I don't like the sound of this at all.

BOBBY: Listen Mamma, I've met a girl here.

MOIRA: I've met the most wonderful man.

MAMMA: But I have begun talks with the Naoroji family – you remember Milly? She's graduated now.

CLIVE: What sort of a man?

BOBBY: I am married Mamma.

MOIRA: We got married this morning.

There is silence from both MAMMA and CLIVE.

BOBBY: We had to get married as soon as possible.

MAMMA: How could you?

CLIVE: Does your mother know about this?

BOBBY: Mamma… I am a grown man. I can make my own decisions…

MOIRA: No, Mother doesn't know.

CLIVE: Who is this man?

MOIRA: Bobby.

MAMMA: What is her name?

BOBBY: Moira.

MAMMA: Parsi?

BOBBY: No, she is from here.
  We want to come and see you together.
  You will love her Mamma. She is clever and sweet and beautiful and she's going to have our child.

MOIRA: He's Indian…a doctor…

CLIVE: You married a darkie?

MAMMA: I don't want to meet her, nor does your father.

BOBBY: Mamma, don't be like that. I know you would have liked to do the whole ceremony, but we can do something when we come…

MOIRA: What does it matter where he's from? I love him.

CLIVE: Listen to me, you stupid cow. I don't want to meet him, I don't want to see him and I certainly don't want to have anything to do with you.

MAMMA: Get rid of this wife and the child.

BOBBY: How can I?

MAMMA: You're a doctor and a man – babies can be flushed out. Wives can be abandoned. When you have discarded this foreign woman, then come home and we will forgive you and it will be forgotten.

BOBBY: *(Horrified.)* Mamma…

CLIVE: You're no daughter of mine. And if you have any bastard black children, don't even try to bring them here.

MAMMA: We do not marry out. Until you have sorted yourself out – don't come home.

BOBBY looks dismayed. He turns and looks at MOIRA. He tries to cover his anguish but she can see.

MOIRA: My father…he said terrible things…he…

BOBBY: My parents are dead.

BOBBY and MOIRA gaze at each other in sadness from opposite sides of the stage and then exit.

SCENE 11

MATTY is shaving BOBBY's face in the nursing home.

MATTY: Keep still Gramps. Going to make you look like a Bollywood star.

BOBBY: Dilip Kumar.

MATTY: Yes. Dilip Kumar.

MATTY quickly and adroitly shaves his grandfather. It takes real time but is done lovingly. BOBBY seems to relax and enjoy it.

MATTY: Used to shave Dad. It was a weird Sunday morning ritual we had. Sort of male bonding. Dad is so hairy. Like a werewolf! Had to steam his face first to soften the hairs. But you're much easier Gramps.

MOIRA enters. She stops and watches, smiling.

I don't have much on my face yet. Only have to shave once a fortnight.

MATTY finishes off by drying BOBBY's face.

MATTY: Wait, gotta do the finishing touches.

MATTY splashes some eau de cologne on his hands and then pats it all over BOBBY's face.

MATTY: Nice and fresh eh? And you smell good. Gran won't be able to resist you.

BOBBY giggles.

MATTY pulls out the photo of BOBBY as a baby. He thinks about it and then shows it to MOIRA.

MATTY: Look, Gran I found this.

MOIRA walks across and looks at the photo.

MOIRA: That's Bobby and his mother. Show it to him.

MATTY: Is that a good idea?

MOIRA: Why not?

MATTY shows the photo to BOBBY.

MATTY: Gramps, who is this in the photo?

BOBBY looks at the photo. He smiles sadly.

BOBBY: Mamma.

MATTY: Is that you?

BOBBY: Mamma…and me.

MOIRA and MATTY watch BOBBY's reaction as he gets upset.

BOBBY: Surely blood is thicker than religious dogma? Surely love is more important than stupid rules? And happiness? What about that? Are we to live our lives according to someone's pronouncements from deep history?
How do we progress as human beings if we live in the past?

MATTY: Is that what happened Gramps? Were you rejected? Is that what your family did?

BOBBY: Mamma said terrible things about you Moira. I never told you. Terrible things about Rosa who grew within you. I couldn't forgive.

MOIRA holds BOBBY's hands.

MOIRA: And my dad said the most dreadful things about you. It didn't seem worth sharing them. But it left a wound didn't it?

MATTY leaves his gran and gramps together and exits.

MOIRA: I hope you always recognise me Bobby.
And even if you don't, I hope there's something somewhere that recognises that I'm an old friend.

BOBBY nods.

MOIRA: We had a good life together. A happy, busy life with our daughter and grandson. You lost your parents, I lost mine. But we had each other didn't we?
That's all we needed.
And work and good friends.

BOBBY: Friends?

MOIRA: A lot of them gone now. It's the end of our era. But I can look back and see the happiness you brought me. I always loved you. I still do.

BOBBY: You have a good face Nurse Murdoch.

MOIRA: Thank you.

BOBBY: You know I can read palms?

MOIRA: Yes, I know, you're good at that.

BOBBY takes MOIRA's palm and looks at it frowning.

MOIRA: What do you see?

BOBBY continues to frown.

Is there a future?

BOBBY: I see a field of grass, a bench and you with sunflowers all around you. Your face is shining.

MOIRA: That's nice.
No tall dark stranger?

BOBBY: A shadow…

BOBBY looks away sadly.

BOBBY: Moira, will you tell me something? Was I a bad man?

MOIRA: No! Why do you think that?

BOBBY: I should not have hidden who I was.

MOIRA: You were a good man, a great father, a loyal husband, a caring doctor. You did more good than bad.

ROSA enters with MATTY, they are carrying some clothes.

ROSA: Look Dad, look!

MATTY: I was talking to my dad over the weekend and he got this off the internet.

ROSA opens up the parcel. She pulls out a Parsi outfit and a little hat.

ROSA: It's a traditional male Parsi outfit. Mike sent it for you. What do you think?

BOBBY takes the outfit and holds it against himself. He fingers the fabric and the embroidery.

MOIRA: Beautiful stitching.

ROSA: Exquisite isn't it?
Do you want to try it on?

BOBBY has already started to strip. ROSA and MOIRA help him into his new outfit. They are all excited.

Eventually dressed, BOBBY places the hat on his head. He admires himself in the mirror. He looks like a traditional Parsi man.

He looks up at the circeau as it is lowered.

MOIRA: Bobby, what are you staring at?

BOBBY: The door is opening again.

MATTY: What door?

ROSA: He keeps talking about a door.

BOBBY wanders towards the circeau.

MOIRA: Where are you going Bobby?

BOBBY: You can't come with me. I'm sorry, but only I can go through it.

ROSA: Dad, there's no door.

BOBBY embraces ROSA and MATTY, then he takes MOIRA's hands in his, turns them palm upwards, kisses them both tenderly and then climbs into the circeau.

MOIRA watches him go sadly.

ROSA: Mum?

MOIRA: I don't think he's coming back this time. Not the Bobby that we knew anyway.

BOBBY turns back one last time to look at MOIRA and then steps through the circeau into 'Alzheimer's world'.

The End.

OTHER TANIKA GUPTA TITLES

Wah! Wah! Girls: A British Bollywood Musical
9781849431873

Fragile Land
9781840023671

Inside Out
9781840023527

Meet the Mukherjees
9781840028614

Tanika Gupta: Political Plays
Gladiator Games, *White Boy*, *Sanctuary*, *Sugar Mummies*
9781849432474

ADAPTATIONS

The Country Wife
Based on William Wycherley
9781840025163

Great Expectations
Based on Charles Dickens
9781849431224

Hobson's Choice
Based on Harold Brighouse
9781840023831

WWW.OBERONBOOKS.COM

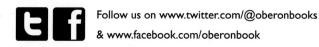

Follow us on www.twitter.com/@oberonbooks

& www.facebook.com/oberonbook